ISBN 978-1-66783-584-6

Ellie's Day at the Zoo

CAROL STORY
PHOTOGRAPHS BY JACK BRADLEY

I first started volunteering at Connecticut's Beardsley Zoo in 2019, so I hadn't been there very long before the Coronavirus pandemic hit and "non-essential" businesses shut down in March of 2020. After a brief period of closure, the Zoo re-opened in several phases, each one requiring facemasks. First they were required both outside and inside, then inside only.

You'll see a couple of references to facemasks in this story. I considered not mentioning masks, but it's such a sign of the times that I didn't want to gloss over it. If you're reading this story to your children in 2042, perhaps you remember having to wear facemasks to the zoo, to the store or to school.

Right now, it's 2022 and we're still wearing facemasks inside, but that won't keep us from celebrating the Zoo's 100th anniversary! As the Zoo itself posted on social media in January 2022:

"In 1922, the Zoo began with a donation of 18 birds and some Barnum circus retirees. Today, Connecticut's Beardsley Zoo is a state of the art, accredited, non-profit facility working year-round to care for more than 100 species –including some who are critically endangered, and potentially facing extinction. We inspire stewards of all ages to help ensure a positive future for wildlife and wild places."

That's quite a transition over 100 years! I'd like to add that based on my observations, every single employee of the Zoo cares deeply about the animals there – as well as about the welfare and preservation of species in the wild. In honor of that, and to support the Zoo's mission now and in the future, all proceeds from this book will go to Connecticut's Beardsley Zoo.

Jack Bradley provided all photographs for this book free of charge. All of the animals in the photographs are or were residents of Connecticut's Beardsley Zoo.

Carol Story, January 2022

One day, Ellie and baby sister Hannah visited Carol at her house

Baby cousin Natalie was also there, and Ellie wanted to get out!

Too many babies! Ellie sighed. Can we go to the zoo?

I know you volunteer there; can I please go with you?

Carol said Why Ellie, you couldn't know me any better!

Let's go! But first please grab your facemask and a sweater

Lots of the animals like it when the air's a little brisk

And the facemasks will help protect us all from the pandemic risk.

On their way to the zoo they had a conversation

All about the animals and how we can help with conservation

Ellie said, I know many animals are endangered in the wild

And Carol replied Ellie, you're quite wise for so young a child!

People have done a lot of things that led to this condition

But now that we know better we can make fixing it our mission!

And that's what people throughout the world are all trying to do

One of the places we see that at our local zoo!

The first creature we will meet is the majestic Andean Condor

They're really big with 10-foot wings and they can really soar!

They live down south in the Andes mountains that really are quite high

The condors soar above the peaks – the rulers of the sky!

Now here we have some Mexican wolves, as you see here, there are three

The first place you can look for them is here, under this tree.

They mostly live in New Mexico and also Arizona

Unless they're in a zoo, you won't find them in Tacoma!

See these guys? These are Red Wolves and they are very rare
If you look for them in the wild, you will not find them there.
I hate to say how few live out there; right now it's less than twenty
Zoos are trying to change that and we hope someday there'll be plenty.
We hope that Kawoni and Peanut here will become a mom and dad
Their pups could help to save their kind. Then wouldn't we be glad!

Look, here's a Maned Wolf! He looks like a long legged fox

And look what he's wearing on his legs – they're extra-long black socks!

And here we have the Rheas, South America's flightless birds

They're right here by the Peccaries, who look like pigs, and live in herds!

(Clockwise, from top: Maned Wolf, Chacoan Peccary, Greater Rhea)

Here's the Giant Anteater. Her tongue is two feet long!

What do you think they eat? If you think Ants! You are not wrong.

They have long sharp claws to open anthills (they must think ants are sweet)

Then they gather ants up with their tongues! Did you know they don't have teeth?

And mother Anteaters, well they have this ingenious knack

For carrying around their babies – they just use their back!

Here we come to the Prairie Dogs, they are just so cute!

Look at them sitting there by their holes in their brownish suits.

Every so often you might hear one give off a loud chatter

The rest of them will sit right up to see what is the matter.

That chatter warns the colony that danger is about

So they go down into their burrows until it's safe to come back out.

Next we have two Bison, or some call them buffalo

They are quite big but don't you ever think that makes them slow!

They live in herds and can run fast. And they even jump

But when they lie down, you will see they look like great big lumps.

They came around the corner and Carol said, Ellie, Hey! Come on!

And meet our wonderful Red Pandas; their names are Berry and Rochan.

It's hard to know the best time for what I call Red Panda peeping

They like to do what they're doing now – of course, they're sleeping!

They're active most at dawn and dusk, just like sometimes you are

There's a great word for that behavior – and that word's crepuscular!

Ellie giggled. That's not me, I am not like that!

But I know someone who is – it's Guinevere, my cat!

Before we head off to the leopards, let's see our White-naped Crane McDuffy

And there's his lovely mate Cora. You'll notice they're not fluffy.

But did you know that cranes all over, well, they love to dance?

They jump and bow and run and flap. They might even prance!

We have two Amur Leopards here; the spotted one's Orion

If I tell you he's one handsome cat, I surely won't be lying!

And here's his sister Kallisto, she's black and has no tail

But please don't think that being tailless means that she is frail.

That thought is quite wrong, you see. If she heard that she would frown

If she was hunting for her food, she could really take prey down!

Both of these leopards are very strong and they represent their kind

If you were to call them beautiful I don't think that they would mind!

And here we have our River Otters, they really like to play

They like to swim and play and eat and swim some more all day!

Check out the Alligators as we head to see our bird most regal

His name is Kodiak and he's our resident Bald Eagle!

(Above: North American River Otters. Facing Page: Bald Eagle, American Alligator)

Here's our Amur tiger ChangBai. Isn't she a lovely sight?

She's pretty! Ellie exclaimed. I love her face, her teeth, her stripes!

Carol said, We had more tigers; yes we had two others

Reka and sister Zeya were born here; ChangBai is their mother!

Where are Reka and Zeya now, asked Ellie, Where else could they go?

Well, they're all grown up now; in the wild they'd be alone.

So for Reka and for Zeya it was time that they moved on

They're each at other zoos now, and we hope they'll both be moms!

Well, said Ellie, it's good for tigers to have more babies so their kind can thrive

They're endangered, so we should help make sure that they survive.

Well, exactly! Carol said, Once again you show your wisdom

And I love it that you are so filled with optimism!

Pictured: ChangBai

To the Rainforest! Ellie exclaimed. To see the ocelot

Put on your mask because I just have to see the sloth!

I know the Rainforest is enclosed and so the zoo has to ask

For us all to help protect the animals – that's why we put on masks!

Carol said, rainforests have diversity, with wildlife of all sorts

They have animals and birds, frogs, snakes and bugs, and lots of plants, of course.

There are lots of animals in the rainforest and you may have heard

It's sad to say that lots of them are known to be endangered.

(Below: Brazilian Ocelot)

Here's our emerald tree
boa (that's a snake)

He's very still; he barely
moves. But I promise –
he's not fake!

The vampire bats are
hard to see; they hang
down from the ceiling

But when you see
their little faces, some
people think that they're
appealing!

(Top: Boat-billed Heron; Bottom: Scarlet Ibis)

If you like exotic birds, well, you surely are in luck

We have Scarlet Ibis, Boat-billed Herons and several kinds of ducks!

And also a strange salamander. Can you say "AX-O-LOT-L"?

We also have a Mata Mata – that's a real cool turtle!

We have Spider Monkeys, Howlers and Pale-faced Sakis, if you please

And Golden Lion Tamarins (but we call them GLTs).

And the Goeldi's Monkeys would just love to meet you

They jump right on fence because they want to greet you!

(Left: Male Pale-faced Saki Monkey;
Below: Golden Lion Tamarins)

Everyone loves the Two-toed Sloths. We have Rhubarb, we have Hope

But will you get to see them move? If I were a bettor, I'd say Nope!

They just like to hang around; they each have their own spot

Another creature that likes the trees is the Brazilian Ocelot.

(Below: Hoffman's Two-toed Sloth.)
(Facing page, top: Poison Dart Frog; Bottom: Red-rumped Agouti)

We also have a Caiman and we have some Poison Dart Frogs

And a Spotted Amazon River Turtle sitting on a log.

Then we have a funny guy – he is a Red-rumped Agouti

As he scampers around his home you'll see his cute patootie!

Before we leave here let me ask you, Do you have a favorite?

While you think, let's go to the fountain, that's where we can sit.

Gosh, that's a hard one, Ellie said. There are so many here

If I had to choose my favorite, it would take a year!

Well, you don't have to pick just one. You could pick a dozen

So we'll come back here another time and bring your sister and your cousin!

I'd really like that, Ellie said. I want to show them everything

This zoo is great all year long – Summer, Fall, Winter and Spring!

There are more animals at the Zoo than we have told you about here. We missed all the farmyard animals, all the ambassador animals, the birds and the Red-eared Slider Turtles in the aviary, our Gray Fox named Gadget, three White-tailed Deer, Sand-hill Crane Gantry, Barred Owls Mist, Xena and Athena, Turkey Vulture Meatball, Great Horned Owl Ohundum, Harris Hawk Arwen, an Eastern Red-Tailed Hawk and Indian Blue Peafowl Madonna and Penelapi along with a few Guinea fowl that roam freely around the grounds. We also missed all the animals in the Research Station: Eastern Hellbenders, snakes, a legless lizard, turtles, Madagascar Hissing Cockroaches, Vietnamese Walking Sticks and other insects.

We also didn't mention the Andean Bears, which are due to arrive sometime in 2022, but were not here when we told this story.

And if you come to visit, don't miss the historic Victorian greenhouse, which has been on the site since 1898. You can also get some refreshments at the Peacock Café, take a ride on a zoo animal on the carousel or buy a souvenir at the gift shop!

(Facing Page: Barred Owl)

Do You Want to Know More?

There's lots more to know about the animals than we could fit into our story! Here's some more information about some of the animals at the Zoo in early 2022.

Andean Condor

Terasita the female Andean Condor has been at the Zoo since 2012. Condors are huge birds. They are among the largest birds in the world capable of flight. Because they are so large and heavy, they live at high altitudes where the air currents can help them stay aloft.

In the wild, they might hang out with other vultures, such as Turkey Vultures and Black Vultures, which find food mostly by smell. The Condor finds it mostly by sight. The other vultures will find food based on the smell and congregate around it; the Condor then will fly in and start to tear it apart so all the birds can eat their fill. This is called a mutualistic relationship – each bird gets something back from the other.

The Zoo used to have a male Andean Condor named Desmond. Desmond is now in Colombia, soon to be released to the wild (if he hasn't been already)!

Andean Condors are ***Endangered***.

(Facing Page, Top: Male Andean Condor Desmond.
Bottom: Female Andean Condor Terasita)

Mexican Wolves.

There are three Mexican Wolves at the Zoo: brothers Kipper and Marco, and female Pika. Also known as El Lobo, the Mexican Wolf (a subspecies of Gray Wolf) is one of the most endangered mammals in North America. By the mid-1980s, they were extinct

in the wild, with only a few remaining under human care. So it was very exciting when they were reintroduced into the wild in 1998. At last count in late 2021, there was a wild population of 186 individuals in New Mexico and Arizona. That's double the number from five years earlier!

Mexican Wolves are **_Endangered_**.

Red Wolves.

Connecticut's Beardsley Zoo is home to female Red Wolf Kawoni and male Red Wolf Peanut.

Red Wolves were brought to the brink of extinction in the wild due to hunting, trapping, poisoning and extreme competition with coyotes. (In this case, "competition" means they want to live in the same places and hunt for the same food sources.) With the help of zoos and the Association of Zoos and Aquariums (AZA) Species Survival Plan (SSP), wild Red Wolves were captured and bred in zoos. In 1987 a reintroduction program was started in North Carolina. Connecticut's Beardsley Zoo contributed eight wolf pups, bred at the Zoo, to this reintroduction program.

Although they were once found from central Texas to southern Pennsylvania to Florida, today the only place Red Wolves can be found in the wild is in eastern North Carolina's Albemarle Peninsula.

Red Wolves are **_Critically Endangered_**. There are currently fewer than 20 individuals in the wild.

Maned Wolves

Female Maned Wolf Guapa and her brother Goncalo were born at the Zoo in 2017. Sometimes people say the Maned Wolves look like foxes on stilts, but they are not foxes and despite the name, they're actually not wolves either! In fact, they are believed to be the only surviving canids (dogs) of the late Pleistocene Era extinction in South America (about 12,000 years ago).

They are very shy mammals that keep to themselves under human care and in the wild. There are only about 4,000 Maned Wolves left in the wild, and this number is dwindling due to their habitat being destroyed by farmers.

Maned Wolves are **_Endangered_**.

Giant Anteaters

Male EO, female Pana and their female baby Chili, born at the Zoo in 2021, are Giant Anteaters. They're called "giant" anteaters because they are the largest kind of anteater. They have long, bushy tails and long noses. They're good swimmers and can use their nose as a snorkel!

Their tongues are long and sticky and they can flick them up to 160 times per minute to pick up ants, termites and other insects. They're called insectivores because insects make up their entire diet.

If you see one up close, you'll see that they have very long claws in front. They are so long that when they walk, anteaters curl them up and sort of walk around on their knuckles! They use their claws to tear apart anthills or termite mounds so they can feed on them.

But they never eat the entire ant or termite colony – they always leave enough so the colony can grow big again – and the anteaters can come back for another meal!

Giant Anteaters are **Near Threatened**.

(Left: Mother Giant Anteater Pana with baby Chili on her back.)

American Bison

American Bison Clara and her daughter Eleanor currently live at the Zoo. The American Bison is the national mammal of the United States. Back in the 1800s there were about 50 million Bison in the American West. By 1900 they were nearly extinct but due to conservation efforts, today there is a stable population of American Bison, largely in public lands managed by the U.S. Department of the Interior. Yellowstone National Park is the only place in the entire United States where Bison have always lived, since prehistoric times.

Some people call Bison buffalo, but really Bison and buffalo are different animals. Buffalo live in Africa and Asia, while Bison live in North America and Europe.

Although they are large and look clumsy, they are really quite agile! They can run up to 40 miles per hour and jump as high as six feet. They are also good swimmers. And they are not afraid of a little cold. If you see them in a snowstorm, you'll see that the snow just stays on them – it doesn't melt. That's because their dense winter coat insulates them so

well! And when the snow gets too deep, they just use their huge heads like snow plows to uncover vegetation to eat.

Due to conservation efforts, the American Bison population is currently considered **Stable**. That's something to celebrate!

Red Panda

Red Pandas Berry, a female, and Rochan, a male, currently live at the Zoo. If you visit on a cool or cold day, you might see them outside. They like cooler weather, as they live at high altitudes in the Himalaya Mountains in Asia where it gets very cold, especially in winter.

Here's a fun fact you can impress your friends with: the word "panda" means "eater of bamboo". So it might not surprise you that one of their favorite foods is bamboo leaves – although they do eat other things, like berries, blossoms, plant leaves and bird eggs. On the other hand, Giant Pandas (black and white bears) eat only bamboo. And even though they're both called pandas (because they both eat bamboo), they are not closely related at all. Giant Pandas are a kind of bear, while Red Pandas have no close living relatives.

Red Pandas are **Endangered**.

Amur Leopard

Amur Leopard siblings male Orion and female Kallisto live at the Zoo, having been born here in January of 2019.

Amur Leopards have long legs and their fur is much longer than that of other leopards. The fur allows them to hunt yet still keep warm in the deep snow and cold winters in their home range – the Amur River valley along the China-Russia border.

Orion is a perfect example of a typical Amur Leopard – with black spots and a long tail.

You'll notice that Kallisto appears to have no spots – she is black – and she has no tail. While it looks like she has no spots, in the right light you can see that she actually does have spots. Her black coloration is due to a genetic variation called "melanism." Melanism is a condition that causes the production of extra black pigment. In leopards, melanism is a normal "recessive" trait – much like blue eyes in humans, only more rare. There are only two melanistic black Amur Leopards in all of the United States: here at Connecticut's Beardsley Zoo, and at the San Diego Zoo.

Kallisto is tailless due to an injury at birth – the mother leopard was "hyper-grooming" (she was a little too enthusiastic with her post-natal grooming) and damaged Kallisto's tail. Zoo personnel removed Kallisto and had to amputate her tail, so Kallisto has never had a tail and doesn't seem to miss it!

Amur Leopards are the most **Critically Endangered** big cat in the world. A recent census estimates that there are only 80 to 100 wild Amur Leopards remaining.

(Facing Page, top: Baby Orion. Bottom: Littermates Kallisto, black, and Orion, spotted.)

Amur Tiger

The Zoo's current resident Amur Tiger is female ChangBai (you saw her picture earlier). In November of 2017, ChangBai gave birth to sisters Reka and Zeya, who have since moved on to other zoos as part of the Species Survival Plan (SSP) for Siberian (Amur) tigers.

Amur Tigers are the largest subspecies of tiger. They live in the Amur-Ussuri region of Siberia, northern China and Korea, overlapping areas where Amur Leopards live. All tigers have pale blackish stripes with a distinctive pattern on the face as unique as a fingerprint. Males are generally one-third larger than females. So if you think ChangBai is big, at over 300 pounds, imagine how big a large male would be – the biggest on record was 850 pounds!

Tigers, like all big cats except for lions, are solitary and only come together to breed. Females usually give birth to two or three cubs, which will stay with mom for about two years and then go out on their own.

The Amur Tiger is a ***Critically Endangered*** subspecies of tiger. Approximately 350 of these great cats survive in northern Asia. All tigers are endangered and protected worldwide.

(Baby Zeya (left) and Reka.)

Below: Reka (left) and Zeya.

Golden Lion Tamarin (GLT)

The Rainforest building at the Zoo is home to male GLT Leão, and female Cricket. GLTs get their name from their impressive mane. You have to admit, their mane does look a little like a lion's mane, but that's about all they have in common with real lions. GLTs are a kind of monkey that lives in the treetops in the rainforests of southeastern Brazil. They're small – only 6 to 10 inches not counting their tails, which are even longer than their bodies; up to 15 inches long! They sleep in the hollows of the trees at night and look for food during the daytime. They eat all kinds of things, like fruit, flowers, bugs and bird eggs. And they're very fast! They leap all through the branches and vines in the rainforest.

Golden Lion Tamarins are **_Endangered_**.

Goeldi's Monkey

Montana (or Monty, as we like to call him) and female Jovi are Goeldi's monkeys, another monkey that lives in the rainforests of South America. Like GLTs, they are very small, with long tails. They live in a different part of the rainforest from GLTs. Goeldi's prefer areas where the trees might be a little more spread out and there are lower, shrubby areas. They also stay lower to the ground than GLTs. Instead of treetops, they like to stay within 15 to 20 feet of the ground. They like to stay close together and when they're separated they communicate with a shrill call. You'll hear them do this when you visit the Rainforest building. They are very agile and can leap about 13 feet through the air. You'll see this too, as they seem to fly from their perch at the back of their habitat to the front, where they can watch you.

Goeldi's Monkeys are **_Endangered_**.

(Fulvous Whistling Ducks in the Rainforest building.)

For information about the author, go to: https://store.bookbaby.com/profile/carolstory

You can also follow or contact Carol at:

https://twitter.com/carols5835 or https://www.instagram.com/carols5835/

Information in "**Do You Want to Know More?**" came from the Zoo website and other online sources. You can read about all of the animals at Connecticut's Beardsley Zoo on the Zoo website at: www.beardsleyzoo.org/our-animals.

Many thanks to Jack Bradley, who provided lots of fabulous photographs to choose from. I wish we could include them all.

I have described all the animals and behaviors based on what was known in 2021 to early 2022. Any misleading statements or mistakes of fact are entirely my own.

– Carol Story, January 2022.